MW00585317

Critical Acclaim
FOR *THE NECRONOMNOMNOM*

"Fans of H. P. Lovecraft and the macabre will love *The Necronom-nomnom*. . . . The grimoire's 50 recipes . . . are sure to bring a smile (or shudder) to anyone who reads them."

—*Arkansas Democrat Gazette*

"The name alone sold me, but after digging into the book itself, I'm even more impressed with the recipes and level of detail that author Mike Slater put into *The Necronomnomnom*."   —*Daily Dead*

"You will love this book for all of the gore-filled recipes based on Lovecraft stories, creatures, and characters. The illustrations that accompany each recipe are fantastic. . . . Super creative . . . it's definitely a book you will want for your creepy collection, and it's perfect as a recipe guide for your next Halloween party."   —*FSM Media*

"*The Necronomnomnom* perfectly captures the flavor of Lovecraft's stories. . . . Tasty and unsettling . . . this book would make a fine gift and look pretty cool on a shelf. . . . For those who love Lovecraft or throwing interesting Halloween parties, this is one tome of lore that is both fun and tasty to dive into."   —*Game Industry News*

"Appealing.... Unlike in the real *Necronomicon*, the concoctions in this grimoire are harmless to conjure up. But maybe don't read the instructions aloud ... just to be safe." —*Geeks of Doom*

"When we saw this, we realized instantly it was the kind of product we liked and that you would like.... The inside has the look of an ancient grimoire with stained backgrounds and teems with marvelous illustrations.... Written out by Mike Slater with a kind of manic care that the HPLHS deeply appreciates."
—*H. P. Lovecraft Historical Society*

"A Cthulhu-sized amount of fun.... This beastly book is loaded to Dagon's gills with absolutely stunning illustrations ... a wonder to behold.... Lovecraft aficionados will eat up *The Necronomnomnom* ... literally." —*Horror Fuel*

"Your must-have guide to Halloween-season eats ... a side-splitting romp through Lovecraft's oeuvre of oddities. Punnishingly delightful names ... are sure to please the longtime fan and Lovecraftian neophytes." —*San Antonio Express-News*

"Absolutely hilarious! ... This cookbook looks like a work of art. It's beautiful.... Great detail was put into making the text sound like it is straight out of one of H. P. Lovecraft's stories."
—*This Geek Loves Food*

"Creepy and spooky.... Maybe you're planning a Lovecraft party, or a Halloween party, or you just want a book of spells to read. Either way, you're set with this hefty, well-appointed tome ... [that has] the ability to chill you to the bone." —*The Providence Journal*

"A handsome volume, with a beautiful embossed cover and copious illustrations.... If you're a Lovecraft fan, this is one you'll want to own." —*The Steampunk Explorer*

"Wonderful and fun.... Not only is the cookbook well produced with great art design, but the content is exceptional.... Beautifully done ... this is an excellent cookbook, and if you are a fan of Lovecraft or just a fan of the macabre, you will love this. If you, like me, are a cookbook collector, this is an indisputable classic that is a must-have." —*The Well Seasoned Librarian*

The Carols of Cthulhu

The Carols of Cthulhu

Horrifying Holiday Hymns from the Lore of H. P. Lovecraft

Mike Slater

Illustrations by Kurt Komoda
Mi-Go Wrangling by Thomas Roache

Countryman Press

An Imprint of W. W. Norton & Company
Independent Publishers Since 1923

For information about permission to reproduce selections
from this book, write to Permissions, Countryman Press,
500 Fifth Avenue, New York, NY 10110

For information about special discounts for bulk purchases,
please contact W. W. Norton Special Sales at
specialsales@wwnorton.com or 800-233-4830

Manufacturing by Toppan Leefung Pte. Lte.
Book design by Faceout Studio, Paul Nielsen
Art director: Allison Chi
Production manager: Devon Zahn

Countryman Press
www.countrymanpress.com

An imprint of W. W. Norton & Company, Inc.
500 Fifth Avenue, New York, NY 10110
www.wwnorton.com

978-1-68268-797-0

10 9 8 7 6 5 4 3 2 1

This monstrosity of
corrupted carols, subverted
songs, and polluted poems
is dedicated to the small
group of long-suffering
friends to whom I sent
these horrendous hymns
every year, usually at
the last possible moment;
to the fans and backers
who wanted this to
happen years ago; and to
the editor who believed
now's the time and made
the Powers That Print
see the unearthly light.
Your screams of pun-
induced rage and anguish
nourish me.

"Once more the ancient feast returns,
And the bright hearth domestic burns
With Yuletide's added blaze;"

—*from "Halcyon Days"*
by H. P. Lovecraft

The Naughty List

Introduction

This tome should provide dark chuckles, exasperated sighs now and then, and the synchronized shaking of many heads. The songs contained within it parody the warm fuzziness of the originals by turning them on their heads, critiquing their syrupy tidings of joy by transforming them into lamentations of cosmic doom, which, for many of us, better fit the abject horrors of the holiday season.

This collection isn't firing a volley to declare war on Christmas or Hanukkah. The lyrics themselves attack no one's beliefs. Lovecraft's Mythos exists outside the Judeo-Christian tradition, and for the most part, the lyrics don't reference specific elements of genuine faiths. It's all in fun. If you know a song that could work for a follow-up volume—should such blasphemy ever come to pass—teach me. You never know, I might include it.

In 1997, the project that led to this book started with "The Night of the Black Mass." Printed on a tractor-feed Okidata printer and mailed to maybe a dozen people, it somehow found its way onto the Internet when that abyss of nightmare was emerging from its infancy. Maybe that's what went wrong. I take no credit, and you can prove nothing. But to my horror, working on the book revealed that I hadn't used the full version of Moore's poem. Who knows what unholy, expurgated, Hallmarkian truncation I used? The mists of time and memory conceal all, except when Moore's ghost *definitely* added stanzas to the poem any time that I wasn't looking. I have reworked, expanded, and—thanks to my long-suffering editor's incredibly exacting, nay, demanding skill with, um, actual poetry—greatly improved many of the original lyrics to the point that some have become hardly recognizable from their first incarnations. So if you count yourself among their original recipients, novel thrills await! While I lament what we had to do to that first holiday poem, which in my head will remain as I originally conceived it, it's far better in most ways. Apparently, I'm tone-deaf and rhythm-impaired.

As such, in one or two unavoidable places, you may detect a rhythm that wanders a step from the original. Under penalty of eternal stalemate in a very special kind of hell, my editor—who now also suffers from post-traumatic syllable disorder—said it was OK. Blame him. He fought valiantly for the Good and Right, but none of this might exist if I had a penchant for doing things the right way. The laughs have to come first. (You don't want to know what happens if they don't. But I've said too much.)

Merry, happy, good, blessed holiday season to you, whatever you do or don't celebrate. May these parodies bring you dark joy, wherever you are and whatever you believe.

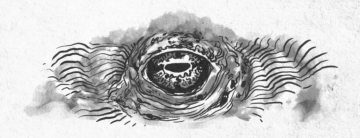

The
Carols
of
Cthulhu

Dark and Knurlèd Ageless Thing

to the tune of "Hark! The Herald Angels Sing"
by Charles Wesley and George Whitefield, 1739, 1961

 Not the voices of heavenly choirs
but shouted refrains of cultists dire.

Dark and knurlèd ageless Thing,
twisted cultists to you sing!
Pieces torn and bodies piled,
Yog, for dinner, eats a child.
Loyal priest in madness writhes,
off'ring up tormented lives,
to accursèd souls lays claim.
O the stars are right again!
Dark and knurlèd ageless Thing,
twisted cultists to you sing!

Woe! What fool unsealed a door?
Lo! What voiced that horrid roar?
   Wakened harbinger of doom
   rising from a sunken tomb,
green in flesh, from 'neath the sea,
baleful ancient deity
   appeased with man, come straight from Hell,
   prisoned 'tween the stars to dwell.
      Dark and knurlèd ageless Thing
      Twisted cultists to you sing!

Jailed for aeons, now released,
quail before their frightfulness:
   blight to life, immortal Things
   risen, borne on bat-like wings.
Not dead, they eternal lie.
With strange aeons, death may die.
   Shorn of chains in their rebirth,
   mourns the subjugated earth.
      Dark and knurlèd ageless Thing,
      twisted cultists to you sing!

The Twelve Days of Darkness

to the tune of "The Twelve Days of Christmas"
by Frederic Austin, lyricist unknown, 1780

No true love or fowl list of items;
instead, this litany that frightens!

On the first day of Darkness,
Cthulhu sent to me
a vision in a dark dream.

On the second day of Darkness,
Cthulhu sent to me
two lurking gugs
and a vision in a dark dream.

On the third day of Darkness,
Cthulhu sent to me
three tombs' ooze,

two lurking gugs,
and a vision in a dark dream.

On the fourth day of Darkness,
Cthulhu sent to me
four ancient words,
three tombs' ooze,
two lurking gugs,
and a vision in a dark dream.

On the fifth day of Darkness,
Cthulhu sent to me
five Elder Things,
four ancient words,
three tombs' ooze,
two lurking gugs,
and a vision in a dark dream.

On the sixth day of Darkness,
Cthulhu sent to me
six cultists praying,
five Elder Things,
four ancient words,
three tombs' ooze,
two lurking gugs,
and a vision in a dark dream.

On the seventh day of Darkness,
Cthulhu sent to me
seven Zanns a-playing,
six cultists praying,
five Elder Things,
four ancient words,
three tombs' ooze,
two lurking gugs,
and a vision in a dark dream.

On the eighth day of Darkness,
Cthulhu sent to me
eight polyps flying,
seven Zanns a-playing,
six cultists praying,
five Elder Things,
four ancient words,
three tombs' ooze,
two lurking gugs,
and a vision in a dark dream.

On the ninth day of Darkness,
Cthulhu sent to me
nine Dark Young prancing,
eight polyps flying,
seven Zanns a-playing,
six cultists praying,

five Elder Things,
four ancient words,
three tombs' ooze,
two lurking gugs,
and a vision in a dark dream.

On the tenth day of Darkness,
Cthulhu sent to me
ten gods a-sleeping,
nine Dark Young prancing,
eight polyps flying,
seven Zanns a-playing,
six cultists praying,
five Elder Things,
four ancient words,
three tombs' ooze,
two lurking gugs,
and a vision in a dark dream.

On the eleventh day of Darkness,
Cthulhu sent to me
eleven pipers piping,
ten gods a-sleeping,
nine Dark Young prancing,
eight polyps flying,
seven Zanns a-playing,
six cultists praying,

five Elder Things,
four ancient words,
three tombs' ooze,
two lurking gugs,
and a vision in a dark dream.

On the twelfth day of Darkness,
Cthulhu sent to me
twelve seals unsealing,
elev—

> IA! IA Cthulhu! Ia! Ia!
> Cthulhu Fhtagn! Ph'nglui
> Mglw'nafh Cthulhu
> R'lyeh wgah'nagl fhtagn!

The Night of the Black Mass

to the tune of "A Visit from St. Nicholas"
or "The Night Before Christmas,"
by Clement Clarke Moore, 1823

A sleepless eve waiting for jolly Saint Nick
transforms our poor witness, left raving and sick.

'Twas the night of the Black Mass, and round the portal
stood nine slaves of Cthulhu and, helpless, a mortal.

The cultists intoned as the victims were slain
in hopes that the Great Old Ones soon woke again.

My mind warped and twisted to witness these sights.
(Unspeakable mem'ries still torture my nights.)

The priest in his cultist robe and I not a scrap
saw something come through with a loathsome wet slap!

The moon hid itself, turning black as a crow,
as all six of the thing's red eyes kindled, aglow.

Arose from the pit diabolical laughter,
and all of those there went insane ever after.

A nightmare appeared from the darkness, I swear,
and, while waving its tentacles, crawled from its lair

with horrific green skin, all so squamous and thick.
I knew in a moment that I would be sick.

It roared and it laughed in a tongue long forgotten,
emitting a stench so unholy and rotten,

all reason devoured as if by a flame,
while the damned priest cavorted and shouted its name:

"O Cthulhu and Yog-Sothoth, Glaaki and Yidhra!
O Cthugha and Nyogtha and Dagon and Hydra!"

From the depths, they all lurched as they heeded his call:
"Awaken, you sleepers, and sweep away all!"

That first one, for me, was much worse than the others.
I caught his attention, far more than his brothers',

and, shaking with fear, into madness I flew
because hiding was hopeless, which clearly he knew.

He turned all his glistering eyes full of doom
upon me, and in them lay all the world's tomb.

He then entered my mind, and he poked all around.
I fell helpless before him, that dark god unbound,

and insanity grew like a hearth gathers soot
into vileness, to which no clear words could be put.

Wings—shrunken, vestigial—drooped from his back,
and beneath his gargantuan bulk, the earth cracked.

Eyes glaringly cruel, red with burst capillaries,
a soul black as ink that an octopus carries,

dank masses of tentacles waved to and fro;
what his mouthparts resembled no mortal could know.

I couldn't quite see if he really had teeth.
Maybe go ask the fish from below Devil's Reef.

I give you this tale, as I write from my cell,
to warn of the horrors called forth by that spell.

That priest ought to have left the book high on its shelf,
what a fool for not knowing he'd claim us himself!

A novice could read what the prophecy said:
The world all would drown in this chaos and dread.

He spoke in a language that drove them berserk,
the cultists all frothing as they did their work.

Enraptured and shuddering madly, they rose
with tendrils and talons for fingers and toes.

Ascending then, skyward, a terrible missile,
he departed, and with him his cadre abyssal.

In the dark, I obey his unspeakable voice
in malevolent dreams, FOR HE GIVES ME NO CHOICE.

Tekeli-li!

to the tune of "O Tannenbaum" or "O Christmas Tree"
by *Melchior Franck, Ernst Anschütz, 1824*

 This caroler faces a different being
than a fir tree, before fearfully fleeing.

"Tekeli-li! Tekeli-li!"
the cry of those so changing,
   a shapeless mass, then eyes appear:
    faint glow of green and madd'ning fear.
"Tekeli-li! Tekeli-li!"
the cry of those so changing.

"Tekeli-li! Tekeli-li!"
From nether caves, you chase me,
   you softened mass, pseudopody,
    you harbinger of misery.
"Tekeli-li! Tekeli-li!"
From nether caves, you chase me.

"Tekeli-li! Tekeli-li!"
it echoes ever after.
    From base to summit, mouths all bite,
    insensate shrieking at the sight.
"Tekeli-li! Tekeli-li!"
it echoes ever after.

"Tekeli-li! Tekeli-li!"
created by the Old Ones,
    but you rose up disloyally
    and thrust them down eventually.
"Tekeli-li! Tekeli-li!"
created by the Old Ones.

"Tekeli-li! Tekeli-li!"
O Shoggoth, ever-changing!
    Your cries pursue me, fleeing fast,
    so I don't end up your repast.
"Tekeli-li! Tekeli-li!"
O Shoggoth, ever-changing!

Silent Knife

to the tune of "Silent Night"
by Franz Xaver Gruber and Josephus Mohr, 1833

In this chill darkness, no heavenly peace
but sacrifices that never will cease.

Silent knife, holy knife,
blade so sharp, blade so bright,
   rounds up virgins soon to defile.
   Stacked so highly the bodies are piled.
Screaming never shall cease!
Screaming never shall cease!

Silent knife, holy knife,
mortals quake at your sight.
   Horrors stream from shadowy stars.
   Blasphemous hosts sing, "Iä! Iä!"
Night eternal is born!
Night eternal is born!

Silent knife, holy knife,
outer gods' furthest night
  mirroring fears from your empty face
  in the cold of the black of space.
Madness covers the earth!
Madness covers the earth!

It Came from out the Midnight Drear

to the tune of "It Came upon the Midnight Clear"
by Edmund Sears, 1849

 No angel sings this verse.
Oh no, it's something worse!

It came from out the midnight drear
    to take the souls we'd sold.
Through angles bent and far from earth,
    it stretched its tendrils cold.
"Beasts on this earth that will torment,
    they serve hellacious Things,"
the book did say in ancient script
    if but these words we'd sing.

Now hard on cloven hooves they come,
   unleashed upon the world
with tentacles and heads of goats
   and wings that they unfurled.
From hellish, dark, and unknown planes,
   they swoop, while still we sing,
and spilling forth from seals unbound
   comes doom's foul Yellow King.

But under sacrificial knife,
   the victims suffered long.
The one we call cannot be lulled,
   a thousand years becalmed,
and man, with war, will stir the pot
   from which all evils spring.
So rush the noise of death and strife,
   and hurry forth our king!

Behold: The days are growing long—
   by twisted monks foretold—
when, with the ever-circling stars,
   comes chaos to enfold
its dread black wings round all the earth.
   Its ancient horrors sing,
and our whole world goes back ere long
   to ageless, evil Things.

I Found It on the Mountain

to the tune of "Go Tell It on the Mountain"
by John Wesley Work II and Frederick Jerome Work or Jennie Lee, 1909

The singer heralds no savior this time
but something better left within the rime.

When I was a seeker,
    I fought 'cross cold and gray.
I searched and bored to find out
    what 'neath the snow might lay.

I found it on the mountain,
frozen in hills its ancient lair.
I lost it on the mountain
from 'fore man's race was born.

It made me a madman,
    awaiting on its call,
and now I only listen,
    pathetic man in thrall.

I found it on the mountain,
frozen in hills its ancient lair.
I lost it on the mountain.
O heed these words that warn.

O Azathoth

to the tune of "Oh Chanukah"
by *Mordkhe Rivesman, 1912*

 Where spun the joyful top in festive bliss,
the Dæmon Sultan whirls in the abyss.

O Azathoth, O Azathoth,
    keep sleeping, you snorer,
so we can party.
    Stay asleep, you horror!
Snooze and keep it stable
    to pipers' mad beat,
universe dreamt up
    from sultan's dread seat.

And while they are playing
    the pipers are thrashing so,
eyes all shut tight, forever in fright,
    and the pipers go mad as they blow.

Eyes all shut tight, forever in fright,
  and the pipers go mad as they blow.

O Azathoth, O Azathoth,
  stay dreaming forever
and do us all a favor by
  awakening never.
Every dream that you dream, that's all that's been.
Mindless floating daemon, sleep through the din.

And nightly, unsightly
  the Outer Gods all round you go,
eyes all shut tight, forever in fright,
  and the pipers go mad as they blow.
Eyes all shut tight, forever in fright,
  and the pipers go mad as they blow.

Barrow of the Hells

to the tune of "Carol of the Bells"
by Mykola Leontovych and Peter Wilhousky, 1919

 What started as a chorus of chanting
ended in mortals bolting and panting.

Dark sunken hells,
stones black and fell,
  all seem to sway
  down in R'lyeh.

Sleepless with fear,
end drawing near,
  great wings unfold
  from depths so cold.

Doesn't belong,
angles all wrong,
  Blasphemous Thing's
  mind shattering

all dreams, and hear
thoughts commandeered.
   Out of his lair,
   lord of nightmare

opens the mound,
flies from the ground,
   rending the veil.
   Loose from their jail,

death they will bring
to everything,
   from realms so drear,
   shambling, and queer.

     Hurry, hurry, hurry, or they'll get us!
     Hurry, hurry, hurry, or they'll get us!

O they descend!—
spawn without end,
   and I'm alone
   but for this tome.

Dark sunken hells,
stones black and fell,
   all seem to sway
   down in R'lyeh.

Sleepless with fear,
end drawing near,
   great wings unfold
   from depths so cold.

Doesn't belong,
angles all wrong,
   Blasphemous Thing's
   mind shattering

all dreams, and hear
thoughts commandeered.
   Out of his lair,
   lord of nightmare

opens the mound,
flies from the ground,
   rending the veil.
   Loose from their jail,

death they will bring
to everything,
   from realms so drear,
   shambling, and queer.

     Hurry, hurry, hurry, or they'll get us!
     Hurry, hurry, hurry, or they'll get us!

O they descend!—
spawn without end,
    and I'm alone
      but for this tome.

O they descend!—
spawn without end,
    and I'm alone
      but . . . for . . . *this* . . . tome.

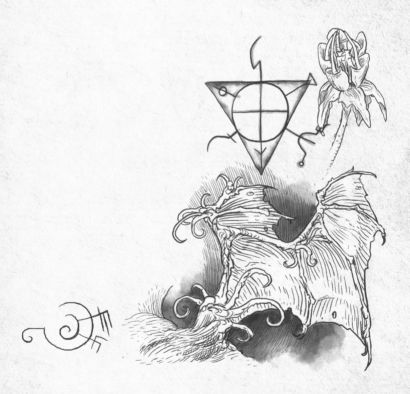

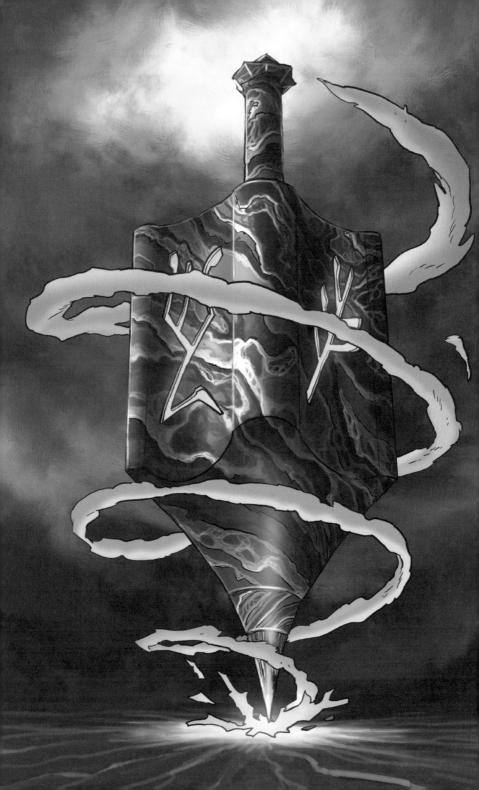

O Dread and Mighty Cthulhu

to the tune of "I Have a Little Dreidel"
by Samuel E. Goldfarb and Samuel S. Grossman, 1927

Behold no spinning young one's toy
but a horror come to destroy!

I had a dire vision
    of madness and decay.
The stars all were aligning
    to open up the way.

O dread and mighty Cthulhu,
    he slumbers in R'lyeh,
and, when he finally wakes up,
    the world will go away!

He has a dragon's body,
  an octopus-like head,
and, if you don't go crazy,
  you'll probably drop dead!

O dread and mighty Cthulhu,
  he sleeps beneath the waves.
His rising we shall hasten
  so we can be his slaves!

These are the stranger aeons
  Alhazred prophesied.
Arise now, O great Cthulhu,
  for death itself has died!

O dread and mighty Cthulhu,
  Iä! Iä! He wakes!
The Great Old One arises!
  The seal, the seal—it breaks!

I Know the King in Yellow

to the tune of "I Have a Little Dreidel"
by Samuel E. Goldfarb and Samuel S. Grossman, 1927

A cultist calls the name herein
to help the end of time begin.

I know the King in Yellow,
    whose name you should not say.
The ritual is ready,
    so let's begin to slay!

"O Hastur, Hastur, Hastur!"
    I'll scream it night and day.
My dagger hand is steady,
    no reason to delay!

So soon he shall incarnate,
    his robes in shreds and thin,
behind him trailing madness
    and tentacles within!

"O Hastur, Hastur, Hastur!"
    I'll scream it night and day.
My dagger hand is steady,
    no reason to delay!

My Yellow King is playful.
    He makes us dance and spin.
To you, it may seem dreadful,
    but this is how I win . . .

"O Hastur, Hastur, Hastur!"
    I'll scream it night and day,
and, when my king is ready,
    bring madness and decay!

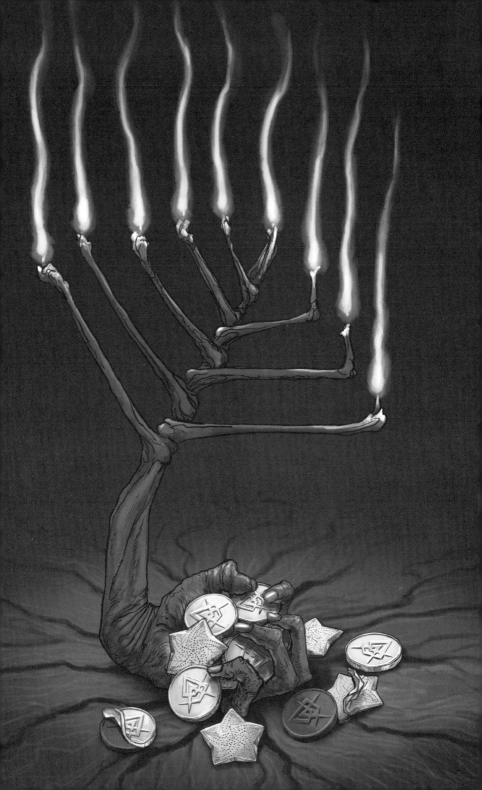

Yog-Sothoth Is Coming. Bow Down!

To the tune of "Santa Claus Is Comin' to Town"
by J. Fred Coots and Haven Gillespie, 1934

 No gifts forthcoming from this entity,
only curses brought forth by zealotry.

He's gonna break out.
    His time has drawn nigh.
You'd better not doubt.
    He won't be denied.
        Yog-Sothoth is coming. Bow down!

Awakened, he's pissed,
    so heed my advice.
You're gonna find out:
    We all pay the price.
        Yog-Sothoth is coming. Bow down!

He hears you when you're chanting,
    His bonds disintegrate.
The stars have gone from bad to good.
    He's the key, and he's the gate!

So you'll scream, and you'll shout.
    Don't look at the sky!
You'll writhe all about.
    The lucky ones die.
        Yog-Sothoth is coming. Bow down!

We wish you'd left him sleeping,
    but, now that he's awake,
it won't matter if you're bad or good.
    There's no fixing this mistake!

No! You'll flop all about,
    and you'll hope to die.
You'll look like a trout
    all covered in eyes.
        Yog-Sothoth is coming. Bow down!

Eldritch Horror's Hand

to the tune of "Winter Wonderland"
by Felix Bernard and Richard Bernhard Smith, 1934

Not dwelling on nature's beauty, this mind
describes a landscape of a darker kind.

Fey bells ring.
 I hear . . . whistling?
In my brain,
 tendrils glistening,
  they alter my sight.
  They're pallid and white.
   Puppets on an eldritch horror's hand!

Brain astray,
 thoughts are hampered.
Gone all gray,
 mind has scampered.
  These shapes don't belong,
  the angles all wrong.
   Puppets on an eldritch horror's hand!

From the plateau, we can get to K'n-yan,
 then be chased by Tindalos's hounds.
They'll slay those who tarry in the Dreamlands,
 but you can get away if you dream sound.

Nameless cults
 will conspire
as we scream
 while on fire.
  From space, they will raid,
   quite mad and depraved.
    Puppets on an Eldritch horror's hand!

Then the meadows will be fit for no man.
 Walking forests will consume the towns.
Lost, R'lyeh will rise again, an omen.
 In chaos, all humanity will drown.

Then it snows,
 'thaqua willing.
Where he goes,
 there's a killing.
  We'll wither away,
   our souls a buffet,
    puppets on an Eldritch horror's hand!

Quite Listless

to the tune of "White Christmas"
by Irving Berlin, 1942

Unnerving dreams of a rising R'lyeh
warp a wistful song of the holiday.

I'm dreaming, but I'm quite listless,
   just like strange aeons long ago
      where the towers glisten,
      and logic's missin'
   amidst angles wrong below.

I'm dreaming, but I'm quite listless.
   With every viscous, passing night,
   may your dreams be tortured with fright,
   and the stars all finally be right.

I'm dreaming, but I'm quite listless,
   just like strange aeons long ago
      where the towers glisten,
      and logic's missin'
   amidst angles wrong below.

I'm dreaming, but I'm quite listless.
   With every cultist chanting rites,
   may your screams for mercy ignite
   and the stars all finally be right.

Evil Tome of
Darkness

to the tune of "I'll Be Home for Christmas"
by Walter Kent and Kim Gannon, 1943

Not a singer who's longing for home
but a madman enslaved by a tome.

There's screaming tonight
in a place I love
all because I have bargained with you.
I'll tell what I know,
knowledge foul and black,
and yet it's true—

Evil tome of darkness
has devoured me,
eldritch glow and dreams of woe,
its presence haunting me.

Hellish pages bind me
  when the witch-light gleams,
evil tome of darkness
  invading all my dreams.

Evil tome of darkness,
  my soul claimed by thee,
blood will flow and pool below
  the crescent blade in me.

Darkest grasp entwines thee
  when your pages scream.
Evil tome of darkness,
  you promised power supreme!

Wretched Foe!

to the tune of "Let It Snow!"
by Jule Styne and Sammy Cahn, 1945

Where falling snow brought holiday cheer,
we heed with dread Time's hands drawing near.

O the nether outside is frightful,
full of creatures fell and spiteful
   all planning our endless woe.
    Wretched foe! Wretched foe! Wretched foe!

O Time's arrow, there is no stopping,
or those cultists' evil plotting.
   Behold the gates' baneful glow.
    Wretched foe! Wretched foe! Wretched foe!

When the rituals all are right,
   all the horrible acts we perform
summon those from beyond the night,
   chittering things in a swarm!

73

As humanity's slowly dying,
and nobody's tears are drying
   Time, so pitiless, just won't slow.
   Wretched foe! Wretched foe! Wretched foe!

When we finally see our plight,
   how we'll mutate, decay, and transform,
and—beg, cry, or pray, though we might—
   no one can say we weren't warned!

O the stars all are aligning,
and so soon they'll all stop shining,
   Ruthless, Time lands the final blow.
   Wretched foe! Wretched foe! Wretched foe!

Tsath'ggua the Frog-Faced Godling

to the tune of "Rudolph, the Red-Nosed Reindeer"
by *Johnny Marks, 1949*

No magical herd of ruminants here,
this leaping creature deals only in fear.

You know Dagon and Hastur and Ith'qua and Nyogtha,
Abhoth, Shudde M'ell, Yig, and Cthulhu,
    but do you recall
      the most heinous godling of all?

Tsath'ggua the frog-faced godling
    didn't really have a nose,
and if you do behold him,
    O the horror only grows.

All of the other Old Ones
	dance around and call the name
of Az'thoth who ignores them
	'cause he's blind, asleep, insane.

You can try to disbelieve.
	Wander through N'kai.
Deep and red-lit caves entice.
	You'll wind up a sacrifice!

Then none will ever find you
	even on a Byakee.
Tsath'ggua will simply eat you,
	damned for all eternity!

Shoggoth the Formless Horror

to the tune of "Rudolph, the Red-Nosed Reindeer"
by Johnny Marks, 1949

The ungulate wanted to serve under reins,
but these forms that undulate threw off their chains.

Shoggoth, the formless horror—
    shapeless, shambling, shrieking thing—
beasts made for mindless labor
    till they overthrew their kings.

All of the other horrors
    made to serve the ancient names
would never help the Shoggoths
    throw off all the Old Ones' reins.

Then one Shoggoth did conceive
  slyly of a way.
    Freedom from those chains so tight:
    Off, the Old Ones heads they'd bite!

Then how the Old Ones feared them,
  and their cities they did flee.
Shoggoth, the formless horror
  ravenous, demonic, free!

Sunken Hells

to the tune of "Silver Bells"
by Jay Livingston and Ray Evans, 1950

In that mortal city, merry bells chimed,
but here horrors wait below the sea slime.

Great Cthulhu, how we miss you,
  waiting such a long while.
In his lair, there's a seal holds him shiftless.
Star-spawn laughing, mouthparts rasping,
  horrors mile after mile,
and now every black corner is queer.

Sunken hells, sunken hells
oozing black slime, ancient city,
gibbering elder thing—
soon will arise dread R'lyeh!

Things from black nights, called by dark rites,
blink with eyes red and green.
They will rise tall as homes in their measure.
Here the bones crunch, cities as lunch
Trumpets herald doomsday,
and below all the waves they yet leer.

Sunken hells, sunken hells—
prisoned by Time in their city,
slavering, twisted things—
soon will arise dread R'lyeh!

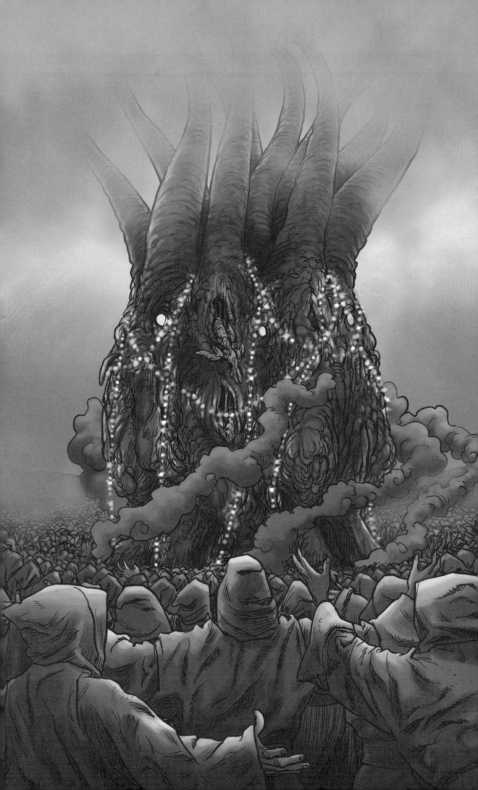

It's Beginning to Look a Lot Like Mythos

to the tune of "It's Beginning to Look a Lot Like Christmas"
by Meredith Willson, 1951

The signs you might expect this time of year
have been usurped by Things horrid and queer!

It's beginning to look a lot like Mythos
    everywhere, Mi-Go.
        Take a look in the poisoned fen
        festering once again
    with fungi strange that rearrange their glow.

It's beginning to look a lot like Mythos.
    Books are full of lore,
        but the scariest tome to see
        is the package that'll be
    at your own front door.

A gnarl of quivering roots
and a beaked maw that hoots
   are the spawn from forest and den.
Boughs that'll talk
and will go for a walk
   are the smallest challenges then,
and cultists cruel can hardly wait
   for Her to rise again!

It's beginning to look a lot like Mythos
   everywhere, Mi-Go.
      Summoned forth by ancient spell,
      dark as her young as well
the evil kind that drips green slime, you know.

It's beginning to look a lot like Mythos.
   Soon the veil will part,
      and the Things that'll make you scream,
      as from portals they do stream,
   so the end will start.

It's beginning to look a lot like Mythos
   Books are full of lore,
      but the scariest tome to see
      is the package that'll be
   at your own front door.

That You, Rhan-Tegoth?

to the tune of "'Zat You, Santa Claus?"
by Jack Fox, 1953

Happily hoping for gifts from a jolly old elf
turns to dreading a visit from an Old One itself.

Shows I'm preparing
for the public sharing,
   pulling off the cloth—
      Whisp'ring and mocking,
        was that something walking?
     That you, Rhan-Tegoth?

Door locked, quite stout;
ain't got no escape route—
   strokes of a distant clock.
      Chains will inhibit
      fleeing the exhibit.
     That you, Rhan-Tegoth?

Are you wringing out victims for me,
so unpleasantly present near me?
   "Wake, great Old One, and rise!" we implore,
    keeping your hideous mouths off the door.

Stomachs are growling—
are you out here prowling?
   I can sense your wroth.
     Wakening draws nigh,
     summoned by an ally.
   That you, Rhan-Tegoth?

Banging and knocking
on the door that's blocking—
   That you, Rhan-Tegoth?
     I am counting the minutes
     while you sunder all the rivets.
   That you, Rhan-Tegoth?

Hear my mantra and honor my prayer.
O stop squeezing me like a nightmare,
   hungry for mortal flesh on which to graze,
    and then for the Old Ones you'll open the ways.

Yet I can't seal ol'
Rhan-ty with the keyhole.
  You can't put him off.
    Behold, three dead eyes leer.
    (One shriek, and I'll die here!)
  That you, Rhan-Tegoth?

Please, please,
I'm on my knees.
Come on through, Rhan-Tegoth!
You're quite a sight—

Do You Fear
What I Fear?

to the tune of "Do You Hear What I Hear?"
by Noël Regney and Gloria Shayne, 1962

 These throats don't sing the birth of the Messiah
but warn us of old gods and new pariahs.

Said the Arab to the little man,
    "Do you flee what I flee?
Drawing ever nigh, little man,
    you can't see what I see—
        a claw, a claw tearing through the veil,
        with a maw as big as a whale!"

Said the little man to the foolish boy,
    "Do you fear what I fear,
reaching through the sky? Foolish boy,
    do you fear what I fear?
        So wrong, so wrong—burning eyes of three
        bringing doom for you and for me!"

Said the faceless god to the Yellow King,
   "Do you sow what I sow
in Carcosa wan, Yellow King?
   Do you sow what I sow?—
      Despair, despair, chaos taking hold.
      Let us watch their ending unfold."

Said the Thing to the people in its lair
   "Rise up, Father Dagon!
Mutate all the people everywhere!
   Rise up, Father Dagon!
      He dreams, he dreams, sleeping in R'lyeh
      He will bring us death and decay."

Father Dagon

to the tune of "Father Christmas"
by The Kinks, 1977

 If you thought those little street thugs were evil,
wait till you see homicidal fish people.

When I was young, I discovered Cthulhu's cult,
  and I wished he was my dad,
and I would hang all the victims at solstice.
  Open those peasants, and I'd go mad.

But the last time I prayed, Father Dagon,
  I stood a monolith on the shore.
A gang of feds flew over and bombed me
  and dropped depth charges at our door.

We prayed:
Father Dagon, give us your blessing.
  Change us all into fish-gilly boys.

95

We'll mate with humans from all the world over.
　　When we have bred, then we'll all make some noise.
　　Those are our ploys:
　　more bipedal half-kois.

Please give my brother a sleek, fishy mouth slit.
　　Please make my sister a sea strigoi.
We just want some crab claws that are monstrously scummy.
　　We'll crawl ashore and then destroy!

Father Dagon, give us your blessing.
　　We'll drown the humans in your inky void.
Father Dagon, give us your blessing!
　　Don't mess around with frilly crinoids.

But make the crawdaddies huge because that's fun!
　　They'll strike when the tides recede.
But if you've got one, please fin me a speargun
　　so I can spike all their shoes to their feet.

Father Dagon, give us your blessing.
　　We'll make the time for your fishy joys
We'll crush the mouthbreathers all the land over.
　　Give all your crumbs to us gilly fish boys.
　　Those are our ploys,
　　your bipedal half-kois.

Give yourself up. Gain immortal fishness.
Trade your skin for scale slime,
but remember the squids who got nothin'
while you're swimmin' through the brine.

Father Dagon, give us your blessing.
We'll make the time for your fishy joys.
Father Dagon, man's time is over.
We'll drown the humans in your inky void.

Father Dagon, give us your blessing.
We'll make the time for your fishy joys.
We'll crush the mouthbreathers all the land over.
We'll crawl ashore and then destroy.
Those are the ploys
of us gilly fish boys!

We All Know It's Twisted!

to the tune of "Do They Know It's Christmas?"
by Bob Geldof and Midge Ure, 1984

 No pleas here to feed the starving and bereft,
these creatures devour the world, with nothing left.

Abdul Alhazred
In twisted times,
   you will bleed and be afraid.
In twisted times,
they'll blot out light
   while they summon shade,

Charles Dexter Ward
and now our world of many
will become their cosmic toy.
Tendrils go around the world
in twisted times.

Dr. Fenton
Now say a prayer. Pray to the Elder Ones.
The time draws near.

Erich Zann
It does, and we are almost done.
There are worlds outside your frail mind,

Erich Zann & Gustaf Johansen
and they're awhirl with leaden fear,

Gustaf Johansen
when the only time that's coming

Gustaf Johansen & (offworld) Erich Zann
is the ending of our years,

Gustaf Johansen, Joe Slater & (silent) Erich Zann
and the twisted knells that ring there
are the blaring trumps of doom.

Randolph Carter
Yes, tonight the gods are going to harvest you!—

Rhan-Tegoth and George Rogers
and the winds will warm Antarctica
in twisted times.
The greatest rift will split it like a knife.

The Necronomicon & von Junzt
Where ancient shadow roams
and madmen read from tomes,

cultists & Robert W. Chambers
we all pray that twisted times befall!

Nyarlathotep
Here's Tulu!

Joe Slater
Now the ending has begun.

Taran-ish
Doom to them!

Joe Slater
Burning till the world's undone,

cultists & Robert Chambers
we all pray that twisted times befall!

cultists
Eat the world!

cultists & Nyarlathotep
Eat the world!

cultists, Nyarlathotep & Abdul Alhazred
Eat the world!

cultists & Robert Chambers
We all pray apocalypse begins!

Nyarlathotep & Abdul Alhazred & Erich Zann
Eat the world!

cultists & Robert Chambers
We all pray apocalypse begins!

The Great Old Ones
Eat the world!

cultists & Robert Chambers
We all pray apocalypse begins!

Last Solstice

to the tune of "Last Christmas"
by Wham!, 1984

 Love for a heart, as originally proposed,
inverts bodily here, with possession imposed.

Last solstice, by fearsome dark arts,
yes, I made you obey,
then sent you away.
With tears,
your rods and your spheres
I'll trap in a living vessel.

Last solstice, I bade you depart.
Though I held you at bay,
you opened the way.
With tears,
again you draw near.
The village thinks I'm the Devil.

Once written, the price high,
    you feign resistance,
but you still must comply.
    "Dwell thee strangely in flesh. I disguise thee!
    Spells to bring you here—in blood, I baptize thee!"

Feeling twisted, I conjured it and sent it,
so devout, praying, "Come! Break through!" and meant it.
    Now you'll know all the ways I've sinned,
    but if you twist my vow, you know you'll still never win.

Last solstice, by fearsome dark arts,
    yes, I made you obey,
    then sent you away.
        With tears,
        your rods and your spheres
I'll trap in a living vessel.

Last solstice, I bade you depart.
    Though I held you at bay,
    you opened the way.
        With tears,
        again you draw near.
The village thinks I'm the Devil.

A shouted rune, fiends with many eyes,
you're hiding from me, and you'll pay the price.
    Old god, here's something to keep a horrid eye on
    Me? It's not that Sent'nel Hill that I'll die on.

Can't face what's discovered
   by my darkest black art.
like Whateley's own mother,
   you'd just tear me apart.
Now I'm bound in this form, you'll never drive me insane.

Last solstice, by fearsome dark arts,
   yes, I made you obey,
   then sent you away.
    With tears,
   your rods and your spheres
I'll trap in a living vessel.

Last solstice, I bade you depart.
   Though I held you at bay,
   you opened the way.
    With tears,
   again you draw near.
The village thinks I'm the Devil.

A face on a pillar
   as the sky splits apart,
a girl for a lover
   with your child to impart.
Maybe, in tears—yes, it will become celestial!

Acknowledgments

My thanks to—

The Dr. Demento Show, to which I listened faithfully on a Philadelphia radio station, ear to the speaker, under the covers, way past my bedtime.

Weird Al Yankovich for opening the way.

Kelly Lee, you know who you are (even if I don't).

All the anguished souls whose beautiful holiday songs I've spent a quarter century gleefully mangling. I'm (not) sorry.

Our original backers for *The Necronomnomnom* and Those Who Believed Again, when we tried to do this as a Kickstarter but the world proved unready. You placed your faith well. Hopefully you've found your patience and continued interest festively rewarded.

Index of Carols

First line of carols appear in *italics*.

Also Available

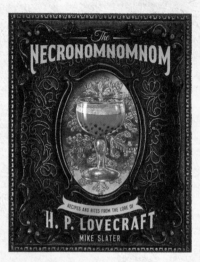

The Necronomnomnom

Recipes & Rites from the
Lore of H. P. Lovecraft

The Necromunchicon

Unspeakable Snacks & Terrifying Treats
from the Lore of H. P. Lovecraft

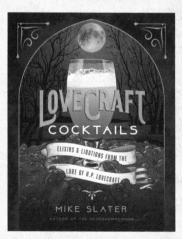

LoveCraft Cocktails

Elixirs & Libations from the
Lore of H. P. Lovecraft